Old Turtle's
90 Knock-Knocks,
Jokes, and Riddles

LEONARD KESSLER

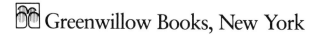 Greenwillow Books, New York

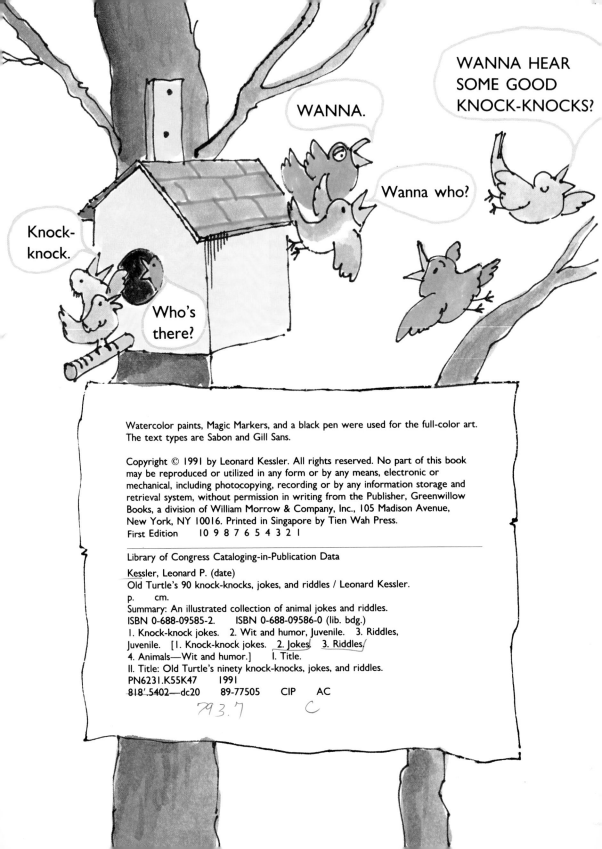

Watercolor paints, Magic Markers, and a black pen were used for the full-color art. The text types are Sabon and Gill Sans.

Library of Congress Cataloging-in-Publication Data
Kessler, Leonard P. (date)
Old Turtle's 90 knock-knocks, jokes, and riddles / Leonard Kessler.
p.   cm.
Summary: An illustrated collection of animal jokes and riddles.
ISBN 0-688-09585-2.   ISBN 0-688-09586-0 (lib. bdg.)
1. Knock-knock jokes.   2. Wit and humor, Juvenile.   3. Riddles, Juvenile.   [1. Knock-knock jokes.   2. Jokes.   3. Riddles.
4. Animals—Wit and humor.]   I. Title.
II. Title: Old Turtle's ninety knock-knocks, jokes, and riddles.
PN6231.K55K47   1991
818'.5402—dc20   89-77505   CIP   AC

793.7   C

To my friends who love
knock-knocks, jokes, and riddles . . .

Matthew Nicholas Kessler, Matthew Orletti,
Matthew and Kara Goldstein,
Eve and Michelle Semins, Syd Robins,
and the kids at Indian Rock and
East York Elementary, York, PA.

"What's wrong with your doorbell?"
 asked Duck.
"It is broken," said Old Turtle.
"Listen. There is no ding-ding
 or ding-dong," he said.
"Then I will KNOCK-KNOCK!" said Duck.

Knock-knock.

Who's there?

ANNIE.

Annie who?

ANNIE-BODY HOME?

"Ha-ha. Very funny," said Old Turtle.

"Annie-body have any more good knock-knocks,
 jokes, or riddles?" he asked.

"WE DO!" shouted Dog, Cat, Rabbit, Chicken,
 Bird, Owl, Frog, Mouse, and Duck.

"Here's one," said Dog.

Knock-knock.

Who's there?

ARF.

Arf who?

ARFLY GLAD TO MEET YOU!

This is a real TWEET.

HOT DOG . . . great to meet you!

Hello to a PURR-FECT friendship.

OWL be your friend.

HARE's to you!

I really HEN-JOY meeting you.

You QUACK me up!

Hi . . . I'm just Old Turtle. Nice to know you!

It's MICE to meet you.

HOPPY to meet you.

Knock-knock.

Who's there?

I. C.

I. C. who?

I. C. YOU ARE HAVING A PICNIC.

Knock-knock.
Who's there?
SARAH.
Sarah who?

SARAH NUFF
FOOD LEFT
FOR US?

MoOoOooo!

Knock-knock.
Who's there?
COWS GO.
Cows go who?
No! COWS GO MOO!

What are we doing?

Making a TV MOO-VIE!

Knock-knock.

Who's there?

SODA.

Soda who?

SODA YOU WANT TO OPEN THIS DOOR?

Knock-knock.

Who's there?

HONEY BEE.

Honey bee who?

HONEY, BEE NICE AND GET ME A SODA, PLEASE.

My puppy was not well.

What did you do?

I took her to the DOG-TOR!

Knock-knock.
Who's there?
ATCH.
Atch who?
HAVE A TISSUE!

Knock-knock.
Who's there?
BOO.
Boo who?
PLEASE DON'T CRY!

Where do ghosts buy their sheets?

At a BOO-TEEK!

Knock-knock.
Who's there?
TANKS.
Tanks who?
TANKSGIVING!

Want a turkey sandwich?

NO TANKS!

Knock-knock.
Who's there?
VCR.
VCR who?
VCR FRIENDS ON TV.

The Old Turtle Show

How about some POP-CORN, Pop?

FROG'S RIDDLES

What do you get if you cross
an airplane and a sausage?

I'll have one
on a pizza!

Answer: A FLYING SAUSAGE!

What would you have if
you dropped a banana
from the top of
the Empire State building?

Answer: A BANANA SPLAT!

What do you get if
you cross a COOKIE and a BURGLAR?

Answer: A CROOKIE!

Why did Frog go to the hospital?

He went for
an HOP-ER-ATION!

14

How did Little Goat stay dry in the rainstorm?

He put on his RAIN-GOAT!

That's GOAT to be the worst joke I ever heard!

What did Frog order at
the fast-food restaurant?

A BURGER AND FLIES!

I'll KETCHUP
with you later!

What do you call
a cashew in outer space?

An ASTRO-NUT!

CASHEW?

Yes.
It's me!

What do you call
a dog in outer space?

BOW·WOW

An ASTRO-MUTT!

What do you call
a little house on the moon?

An ASTRO-HUT!

RABBIT'S JOKES

What do you call
an umbrella that
marches in a band?

A DRUM-BRELLA!

What do you call
an umbrella that does not know
the words to a song?

MMMMM!
HUMMMMM!

Rain
Rain
Go away

HMMMMM!
HMMMMM

A HUM-BRELLA!

RABBIT KNOCKS

Knock-knock.

Who's there?

DON'T CHEW.

Don't chew who?

DON'T CHEW WANT TO FIND OUT?

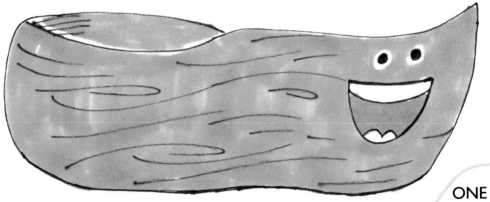

Knock-knock.

Who's there?

WOODEN SHOE.

Wooden shoe who?

WOODEN SHOE LIKE TO KNOW?

ONE SHOE open the door, you'll know!

Knock-knock.

Who's there?

WHEEL.

Wheel who?

WHEEL YOU BE
MY
VALENTINE?

Knock-knock.

Who's there?

WANT.

Want who?

WANT, WHO, THREE, FOUR!

MOUSE'S JOKES & RIDDLES

How do mice race on the frozen lake?

On MICE SKATES!

How do mice pay when they go shopping?

With their MOUSETER CHARGE CARDS!

Why did Little Mouse turn off the TV?

We want Mickey!

He did not want to watch the
A-CAT-AMY AWARDS SHOW!

Mousetronaut: I just got back from the moon.

Little Mouse: Tell me, what is the moon really like?

Mousetronaut: The moon is a great big ball of CHEESE!

Little Mouse: Why did you come back to Earth?

Mousetronaut: TO GET SOME CRACKERS!

What is Mouse's favorite party?

I MOUSE leave before midnight.

A MOUSE-CARADE PARTY!

How do very rich mice go to work?

In LIM-MOUSE-INES!

I have a brother who lives in MOUSE-A-CHUSETTS!

My friend lives on the MOUSE-ISSIPPI.

Where do kangaroo mice live?

In MOUSE-TRALIA!

Hi ya, Mate!

First Mouse: My cousin is a Russian Mouse.
Second Mouse: Where does she live?
First Mouse: In MOUSE-COW!

Enough with the MOUSE JOKES!

DUCK'S JOKES & RIDDLES

Why does Duck's roof
leak when it rains?

Because of all the QUACKS in the roof!

Where do little cows eat their lunch at school?

In the CALF-ETERIA!

Little Calf can play the banjo.
I think he will be a MOO-SICIAN!

Where do musical cows go
to get into Show Biz?

To MOO YORK, MOO YORK!

I'm MOO-VIN
to MOO YORK,
MOO YORK!

How do bulls protect themselves?

They wear BULL-ET PROOF VESTS!

Where do bulls get their messages?

On the BULL-ETIN BOARD.

What do bulls do when they go shopping?

Will that be cash or charge, sir?

They CHARGE!

What do you get when you cross
a chicken and a duck?

She can read the HEN-TIRE book.

Cluck Quack Cluck Quack

You get a very smart bird
who can read the DUCK-TIONARY
and the HEN-CYCLOPEDIA!

CHICKEN'S
RIDDLES & JOKES

How does Chicken mail a letter?

Where do you live?

CHICK-AGO.

Henrietta
To Henry
6 Stoneham
New City, NY
10956-1113

EGGS-
PRESS
MAIL

In a HEN-VELOPE!

How did Chicken get all A's in school?

Henrietta
Spelling A
Writing A
Math A
Art A
Music A
Reading A

She did EGGS-TRA work!

She really sets a good EGGS-AMPLE.

I think I will EGGS-IT on that one!

28

Fly: My best friend won't go out of his house.

Bee: Why won't he go out of his house?

Fly: Because he is a HOUSEFLY!

Doctor, Doctor, Little Pig has a bad rash.

Let's give him some OINK-MENT!

CHICKEN KNOCKS

Knock-knock.
Who's there?
PHILIP.
Philip who?
PHILIP THE TANK
WITH GAS!

I GAS that's OIL you want?

Ha Ha!

Knock-knock.
Who's there?
TENNIS.
Tennis who?
TENNIS MORE
THAN NINE!

ANT that the truth!

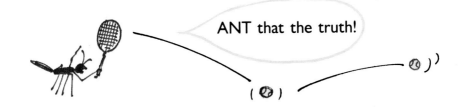

Knock-knock.
Who's there?
CARA.
Cara who?
CARA NUFF TO OPEN
THE DOOR?

Knock-knock.
Who's there?
MINNIE.
Minnie who?
MINNIE-SOTA!

MINI-SODA?

Knock-knock.
Who's there?
ALLIE.
Allie who?
ALLIE-BAMA!

ALI-BABA?

CAT'S KNOCK-KNOCKS

Knock-knock.

Who's there?

PENCIL.

Pencil who?

PENCIL-VANIA!

Knock-knock.

Who's there?

IDA.

Ida who?

IDA-HO!

 IDA who?

 IDA KNOW!

 Wow!

Now, that's a POTATO!

Knock-knock.

Who's there?

CATTLE.

Cattle who?

CATTLE BE HERE

IN A MINUTE.

Knock-knock.

Who's there?

KEN.

Ken who?

KEN YOU COME OUT AND PLAY?

Knock-knock.

Who's there?

WADDLE.

Waddle who?

WADDLE I DO IF YOU

DON'T OPEN THE DOOR?

Knock-knock.

Who's there?

SYD.

Syd who?

SYD DOWN AND TAKE A REST.

Knock-knock.

Who's there?

VANNA.

Vanna who?

VANNA WE GOING TO EAT?

Save some
for your ANT!

Knock-knock.
Who's there?
LES.
Les who?
LES BE FRIENDS.

Knock-knock.
Who's there?
HALF FEW.
Half few who?
HALF FEW GOT
THE TIME?

BIRD-DAY time!

Time for more jokes!

Time out!

Once upon a time!

Rest time!

Show time!

Night time!

Time to go home!

Snack time!

Play time!

35

What has one horn and gives milk?

A MILK TRUCK!

How do cats shop?

FROM A CAT-ALOG!

What's
this?

A CAT-A-LOG!

What day of the week do french fries hate the most?

FRY-DAY!

What do you call a rooster who is a very good cook?

A COOK-A-DOODLE-DOO!

What do you call salad
that is afraid to
come out of the bowl?

CHICKEN SALAD!

BIRD'S
JOKES & RIDDLES

What do you say to a little bird
who is seven years old today?

Have a
pleas-ant
day!

HAPPY BIRD-DAY TO YOU!

Why do birds love Halloween?

BOO!

MEOW!

They can go out and TRICK OR TWEET!

Let me call you TWEET-HEART!

Why did Bird go to the doctor's office?

He went there for a TWEET-MENT!

Can you
KIT me
a Band-Aid?

Kitten: I work for a doctor.

Frog: Then you must be a FIRST-AID KIT!

BIRD'S KNOCK-KNOCKS

Knock-knock.

Who's there?

PASTURE.

Pasture who?

PASTURE BEDTIME, TURTLE.

Sham poo $1⁰⁰

Knock-knock.

Who's there?

CHAMP.

Champ who?

CHAMP-WHO MY HAIR, PLEASE.

Birds don't have hair!

I can't HAIR you!

Knock-knock.

Who's there?

SAUL T.

Saul T. who?

SAUL T. FOOD
MAKES ME THIRSTY!

 What comes after THIRSTY?

 Friday, Saturday, and Sunday!

 That's a WEEK joke!

Knock-knock.

Who's there?

ANITA.

Anita who?

ANITA COLD GLASS OF WATER!

ANITA break from these knock-knocks!

41

OWL'S RIDDLES & KNOCK-KNOCKS

What do you call an alligator
with a bad cold and a runny nose?

AN ILL-IGATOR!

What happens when ghosts get hurt?

They have BOO-BOOS!

What do cowboy ghosts wear?

BOO JEANS!

Knock-knock.

Who's there?

I. M. HOLDEN.

I. M. Holden who?

I. M. HOLDEN MY BREATH

UNTIL YOU OPEN THE DOOR!

 Try to be nice.

 OWL try!

Knock-knock.

Who's there?

KIMMY.

Kimmy who?

KIMMY A HIGH FIVE!

HIGH don't believe it!

43

Knock-knock.
Who's there?
ELLA.
Ella who?
ELLA-GATOR!

Knock-knock.

Who's there?

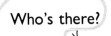

ELLA.

Ella who?

ELLA-VATOR!

Knock-knock.
Who's there?
THEA.
Thea who?
THEA LATER,
ELLA-GATOR!

Knock-knock.
Who's there?
BEN.
Ben who?
BEN HERE A LONG TIME!

Knock-knock.
Who's there?
OWL.
Owl who?
OWL BE HERE
UNTIL YOU OPEN
THE DOOR!

OWL see you later,
OWL-IGATOR!

OWL be back.

"HOLD IT. HOLD IT!"

shouted Old Turtle.

"The doorbell is fixed.

So . . . NO MORE KNOCK-KNOCKS!"

"No more knock-knocks?" asked Frog.

Knock-knock.

Who's there?

I. M. 2.

I. M. 2 who?

I. M. TOO SHORT TO REACH YOUR BELL!

I don't have a bell!

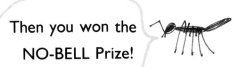

Then you won the NO-BELL Prize!

Ding-dong.
Who's there?
E. I.
E. I. who?
E. I. E. I. . . . O!

Ding-dong.
Who's there?
MARY LEE.
Mary Lee who?
MARY LEE WE SING THIS SONG!

"Oh, Old Turtle,

open that door.

E. I. E. I. . . . O!

With a KNOCK-KNOCK here,

and a DING-DONG there,

RIDDLE-DIDDLE here,

and a JOKE-JOKE there.

Here a knock,

there a knock,

everywhere a KNOCK-KNOCK.

Oh, Old Turtle,

open that door.

E. . . . . I. . . . E. . . I. . OOOOOOOH!"

w

Knock-knock.

Who's there?

RITA.

Rita who?

RITA LOT OF GREAT
KNOCK-KNOCKS,
JOKES, AND RIDDLES
by Old Turtle and his friends.

Other books starring
Old Turtle and his friends:

OLD TURTLE'S RIDDLE
AND JOKE BOOK

OLD TURTLE'S SOCCER TEAM

THE WORST TEAM EVER

THE BIG MILE RACE

OLD TURTLE'S WINTER GAMES

OLD TURTLE'S BASEBALL STORIES

SUPER BOWL